POEMS
New and Selected

POEMS
New and Selected

By

George Mackay Brown

1971

THE HOGARTH PRESS

LONDON

Published by
The Hogarth Press Ltd
42 William IV Street
London W.C.2
*
Clarke, Irwin & Co Ltd
Toronto

ISBN 0 7012 0345 5

Printed in Great Britain by
Redwood Press Limited
Trowbridge & London

TO

ERNEST and JANETTE
MARWICK

Some of the poems in the *New Poems* section have appeared in *The Scotsman, The Listener, Lines Review*, B.B.C. television; and in HONOUR'D SHADE (Chambers) 1959, YOUNG WINTER'S TALES (Macmillan) 1970, THE FIVE VOYAGES OF ARNOR (K.D. Duval) 1966.

CONTENTS

NEW POEMS

THE FIVE VOYAGES OF ARNOR

I, Arnor the red poet, made
Four voyages out of Orkney.

The first was to Ireland.
That was a viking cruise.
Thorleif came home with one leg.
We left Guthorm in Ulster,
His blood growing cold by the saint's well.
Rounding Cape Wrath, I made my first poem.

Norway hung fogs about me.
I won the girl Ragnhild
From Paul her brother, after
I beat him at draughts, three games to two.
Out of Bergen, the waves made her sick.
She was uglier than I expected, still
I made five poems about her
That men sing round the benches at Yule.
She filled my quiet house with words.

A white wave threw me on Iceland.
Sweyn's skull is there (my brother) in a round howe.
Rolf rode him down
In Tingvoe, after the council, and rode on
Through villages, red-hooved, to the sea
Far from Inga his sister
And the lawless cry in the cradle, Inga's and Sweyn's,
And the farm at Rangower.
They put an axe in my hand, the edge turned north.
Women in black stood all about me.
There were lilies and snow on the hill above Broadfirth
And Rangower silent.
In Unst two nights, coming home,
We drank the ale and discussed new metres.
For the women, I reddened the axe at a dog's throat.

I went the blue road to Jerusalem
With fifteen ships in a brawling company
Of poets, warriors, and holy men.
A hundred swords were broken that voyage.

11

Prayer on a hundred white wings
Rose every morning. The Mediterranean
Was richer by a hundred love songs.
We saw the hills where God walked
And the last hill where his feet were broken.
At Rome, the earl left us. His hooves beat north.

Three Fridays sick of the black cough
Tomorrow I make my last voyage.
I should have endured this thing,
A bright sword in the storm of swords,
At Dublin, Micklegarth, Narbonne.
But here, at Hamnavoe, a pillow is under my head.
May all things be done in order.
The priest has given me oil and bread, a sweet cargo.
Ragnhild my daughter will cross my hands.
The boy Ljot must ring the bell.
I have said to Erling Saltfingers, *Drop my harp*
Through a green wave, off Yesnaby,
Next time you row to the lobsters.

OUR LADY OF THE WAVES

The twenty brothers of Eynhallow
Have made a figure of Our Lady.
From red stone they carved her
And set her on a headland.
There spindrift salts her feet.
At dawn the brothers sang this
    Blessed Lady, since midnight
    We have done three things.
    We have bent hooks.
    We have patched a sail.
    We have sharpened knives.
    Yet the little silver brothers are afraid.
    Bid them come to our net.
    Show them our fire, our fine round plates.
    Per Christum Dominum nostrum
    Look mildly on our hungers.

The codling hang in a row by the wall.
At noon the brothers sang this
    Holy Mother, Una the cow
    Gives thin blue milk.
    Where is the golden thread of butter?
    The stone in the middle of our glebe
    Has deep black roots.
    We have broken three ploughs on it.
    Per Christum Dominum nostrum
    Save Una from the axe,
    Our dappled cow with large eyes.

The girls go by with pails to the byre.
At sunset the brothers sang this
    Sweet Virgin, the woman of Garth
    Is forever winking at Brother Paul.
    She puts an egg in his palm.
    She lays peats in his cowl.
    Her neck is long as spilt milk.
    Brother Paul is a good lad.
    Well he brings wine and word to the priest.

But three red midnights
His tongue has run loose among dreams.

Paul has broken knees at the stone.
At midnight the brothers sang this
        Queen of Heaven, this good day
        There is a new cradle at Quoys.
        It rocks on the blue floor.
        And there is a new coffin at Hamnavoe.
        Arnor the poet lies there,
        Tired of words and wounds.
        In between, what is man?
        A head bent over fish and bread and ale.
        Outside, the long furrow.
        Through a door, a board with a shape on it.

Guard the ploughs and the nets.

Star of the Sea, shine for us.

VIKING TESTAMENT

OX

To Thorstein the Ox, I give and bequeath these furrows,
The hawk above, the seal below,
The worn runes over the lintel
    Ingibiorg tallest of women
    carried wine to the traveller
Let the fire watch from the hill, Thorstein.
Scour the axe at the grindstone.
Beat the plough into edges.
I expect Bui from Ireland
Now that his cheek has the bronze curl.
His father opened the quarry.
His father took the hawk on his wrist.
His father sang to the curious seals.
His father had fair dust to lie with,
Ingibiorg, tallest of women.
His father rode down to the ships.
Then one morning
His father lay crooked in seaweed,
A cold man among red swathings.
      Hoof and scarecrow are Thorstein's,
Scythe, flail, quernstones, forge.
So dowered, the ox in the furrows
May quench those Irish axes.
To Helga his wife, ale-kirn and griddle.

DOVE

To the Eynhallow kirk, my fishing-boat *Skua,*
The sail and the oar also.
Erling, our holy prodigal, is there,
Gaunt with heavenly bread.
His net is a bunch of various holes,
A thing of laughter to fish.
Lost in prayer, the hands of the brothers
Are clumsy with ploughshares.
Rooted in praise, their tongues
Compel corn and oil
From the seven ox-dragged seasons.

Their queen is a stone woman,
Their lord a scarecrow with five red tatters.
Mild as a tree of doves,
Bui's wrath is no more to them
Than a painted hawk on a sail.
The net to those long robes
Who call the codling 'little silver brothers'
Even as they suck the bones clean
All the brightening days of Lent.

ROSE
I do not forget thee, my Sigrid.
He carried thee off to Barra
(Thee and thy thirteen Aprils)
Einar thy man. Too soon
That prow unlocked the horizon.
　　　　Thy father is quiet now
Who once bore fire to the castles,
And as for thy brothers, one
Has a skull square as an ox,
And Erling glides in a trance
Through bell and psalm and secret,
A cold mouth in the godstreams.
　　　　What can I leave thee? Thou hast
Horizons of whale and mermaid
Far in the west, a hall,
Three ships in Cornwall and Ulster, trading,
A young son with black curls
And five horses in the meadow.
Arnor has sailed to the quarries in Eday
With chisel and harp.
That stone is red as fire, roses, blood.
I pay well for my verses.
'Cut a deep rune for Sigrid, Arnor'.
Irishmen will read it perhaps
Over a fated lintel,
One fragrant stone among blackened stones.

THE COAT

She bowed in her door, all ripeness.
The reaper went round and round.
Wave after wave of bread
Fell with a secret sound.
She sent the shuttle flying,
She laid the new cloth by,
And through that yellow spindrift
She sent a drowning cry.

With lie and crust and rag
Between two trees we move,
The drifting apple blossom
And the three nails of love.
Naked we come and we go.
Even the Incarnate One
Shed his seamless splendour
Under a sackcloth sun.

The old ploughman of Gyre
Laughed above his ale.
Lie after lie he stitched
Into a masterly tale.
He put down an empty mug.
The thread shore in his throat.
Between crib and coffin
You must dance in a beautiful coat.

CAROL

In the first darkness, a star bled.

The war of cloud and summit, other wounds.
Hills cupped their hands
And the rain shone over knuckles of rock and
            dropped to the sources.
Precious that well-hoard.
The priests gathered in secret jars
Lustrations for the passionate and the dead.

You were blessed, young tree
With one apple.
Far on you must bear the five godwounds,
            prefigured and red.

The deer runs on, runs on, swiftly runs on
Before bird and arrow,
Then bends, obedient to the arrow, its
            branching head.

A hunter's hand has
            broken the wild grape
To stain and seed.

And the hunter's hill opened with a
            green sound,
A stalk of corn,
And the blacksmith took from his forge a
            powerful blade.

Now this, a cry in our atom-and-planet
            night —
A child wailing,
A child's cry at the door of the House-of-Bread.

KIRKYARD

A silent conquering army,
The island dead,
Column on column, each with a stone banner
Raised over his head.

A green wave full of fish
Drifted far
In wavering westering ebb-drawn shoals beyond
Sinker or star.

A labyrinth of celled
And waxen pain.
Yet I come to the honeycomb often, to sip the finished
Fragrance of men.

SEA ORPHEUS

A plough and barley fiddle
For one tide-raped girl
Sang in the looms of the sea.
Driftweed red as lashes
Scored the strings, seals
Clustered around (old salts
They swig shanties like ale,
They shine like bottles.)
      The fiddle
Stretched one thin strand across
The warp of the ebb.
      Eurydice
Caught in the weaving streams
Was half enchanted now
To a cold mermaid.
      The Salt One
Turned the wave round. He gathered
The Song of the Five Seas
Into his loom — Suleskerry
Flashed a new eye, Ahab
Hailed Jonah across
Tumultuous whaletracks, gulls
Climbed up the Glasgow sky
Rivet in beak.
      The Salt One
Had more to do than pity
A sinking mouth, or heed
One mortal cornstalk whispering
A legend of resurrection
Among the spindrift.
      The Salt One
Unrolled webs and bales
Above the drowning.
      Sea girls
Take this buttercup girl
To her salt bridal.

THE MASQUE OF PRINCES

SEA JARL

> Arkol the skald mingled these
> words with harp strokes
> at the Earl's Hall at
> Orphir in Orkney in the
> Yuletide of 1015.

Our salt march ended before the city.
The king said, 'Their roofs are tall.'
We closed the five roads into the city.
They threw down stones from the wall.
Bones were broken, a skull, twelve ribs.
We commandeered fields round the city
And cattle, barns, horses, women, wells.
They threw down fire from the wall.
A skull was charred.
Roofbeams hissed in the Seine.
We circled the wall with dice and wineskin.
The city rotted slowly
Like a spotted corpse in a charnel.
They threw down insult and curse
But that hurt no-one,
The men from the fjords are not sensitive.
Armand the spy reported
Now they were eating rats in the city
And fungus that creeps between stone.
The merchants (said Armand) were poor as the students
And the priests distracted
With shrivings, anointings, requiems.
When the wind lay towards the city
We turned the sputtering ox on the spit.
On the fortieth day the stones were disordered
And Ragnar stood in the gate.
Tapestry. Vats. Opal. Nakedness. Ashes.
The harp was silent. I drew my fingers through silver.
We stayed in the city seven days,
Then dragged carts to the ships at the mouth of the river.
We waited two nights for a wind.

21

I put the siege in a set of formal verses.
The skippers did not praise that poem.
(This is for blacksmiths and poachers.)
We arrived in Jutland in time for the spring sowing
With a cargo of silver, corn, foreign rats.

LORD OF THE MIRRORS

            A dance Bernard of Ventadour
            made, with masks and
            lutes and ladies, for
            the investiture of
            Philip Count of Narbonne
            in April 1130.

The new prince questioned a very ancient shield

    Lord, the first quartering sheweth
    A skull, a sheaf of corn, a mask
    (Your bread is uttered on long sweet throats)

    Prince, the second quartering sheweth
    A skull, a sword, a mask
    (Your soldiers gleam at the five gates)

    Sire, the third quartering sheweth
    A skull, a harp, a mask
    (Poets stain your parchment with nightingale notes)

    Man, the fourth quartering is blank
        'Between skull and mask
        This face, a bright withering flower'

            A breath, surge of cloud,
                through the bronze mirror.

                    *

The new prince goes among roses, cupids, peacocks

        Beast, what is love?
        Phallus, rut, spasm

        Peasant, what is love?
        Plough, furrow, seed

        Priest, what is love?
        Prophecy, event, ritual

        Lord, what is love?
        Lys, and daunce, and viol

        Man, what is love?

23

On the garden pool breezes, a
caul of sackcloth.

*

The new prince kneels at a rood, scarlet and black

Man, where have you been this loud April day?
I followed the hounds to a kill.

Man, what have you done with the royal stag?
Five wounds I bore to a ruined hall.

Man, who received that sacrifice?
A lady, stricken and still.

Man, was there bread on her table?
The rat had devoured the earth-gold. Silent
the stones in the mill.

Man, what lamp in the rafters?
A star that pierced like a nail.

Man, was there fire in that hearth?
Breathings of ox and ass. The lady cried in
the straw. Night laid a shroud on the hill.

That vigil done,
The rood was rose 'of ravissement and ruth'.

*

Now, Mask-and-Skull, rear high among the trumpets!

PRINCE IN THE HEATHER

> The bard Alasdair MacNiall
> made this in Barra
> the day after the true
> prince left Scotland
> for France, 1746.

Who would have thought the land we grew in, our mother,
Would turn on us like a harlot?
The rock where the stag stood at dawn,
His antlers a proud script against the sky,
Gave us no shelter.
That April morning the long black rain
Bogged our feet down
But it did not douche the terrible fire of the English,
Their spewings of flame.
(I think it will rain a long time at Culloden
And steel rot under the stone.)
Who would have thought our own people,
Men of our tongue and lineage,
Would make one wall that day with barbarians?
We prayed our endless mountain tracks
Would baffle the hunters
But the armies marched like doom on the one road
To the one graveyard.
Who would have thought for a moment
But that our leaders had wisdom,
Men skilled in the ancient rites and duties of warfare?
Tinkers from a ditch
Would have directed the lines better that morning.
Casually the cannonball burst those ribs,
Removed that leg.
They harried us like rats from a granary,
A fury worse than dogs.
A great shining thing is gone forever from the glens.
Sheep drift through the halls of the chief and his lady.
The white rose is withered.
Now grandsons of hunter, fisherman, bard
Must turn high courtesy to unction,

A manner and a speech to please the Saxons,
A thing never known before.
Who would have thought our prince, that hero,
While we plucked broken steel from the forge of our valour,
Would take to the screes, a frightened stag?

WHITE EMPEROR

> A troop of irregular soldiers
> led by a woman sing these
> choruses on the road near
> Ekaterinburg, March 1918.

What are you, skeleton with the bayonet?
The Ploughman

What are you, skeleton with rifle and bullets?
The Sower

What are you, skeleton dragging a field gun?
The Harrower

What are you, scarecrow with the knife?
The Reaper

What are you, scarecrow with stones?
The Miller

What are you, shadow among the ashes?
The Baker

*

Unmasked, the Little Father and his children
    Drift on. The sky is red.
Five winters now he has doled us blood and snow
    For our daily bread.

Now in the fifth winter the rat is king
    Of furrow and mill.
That golden mask has worn you, Little Father,
    Down to the skull.

Mane and sabre whirl against the sunset.
    Those princes turn
And fade in the snow. From Omsk to Warsaw, this starfall,
    The Russias burn.

*

Who called us brothers of ox and mule?
Peasants we were,
Children of The White King.

Who calls us skeletons, rags, shadows?
Soldiers we are,
Comrades of The Red One.

We are the people. Forge and field are ours.
I am Natasha.
I measure the sun with lucent eyes.

The inn-keeper at Bethlehem writes secret letters to the Third Secretary (Security) at the door marked with dolphins in the fifth street north from Temple and Dove-market.

Came the first day of the week five guardsmen, Greeks. No sleep in the village for their choruses. Their lamp still burned at sunrise. One broken jar. Rachel's scent was in the sergeant's sheets. Came a troop of merchants, solemn men, with currants in their satchels, they were up and gone early, on four camels, southward. *Who will pay for the jar?* I said to the guardsmen. *Caesar,* said a corporal. *Rachel,* said the sergeant, *she broke it. And anyway,* said a guardsman, *the drink was bad.* God keep me from guests like them. It was this summer's wine, the leaven still moving in it, a little cloud. The Chian and Syrian are for silk purses.

*

These passed through my door yesterday — Jude and Abrim and Saul, farmers. Jude had sold an ox at the mart. *A fire in the back room, a lamp, dice, a skin of wine,* said Jude. An Egyptian with scars on his face, he left the north-bound camel train, he ate barley cakes and fish and was most courteous and laid Ethiop coins on the table. Then Abrim's wife, crying under the stars, *Where is Abrim? He hasn't come home, the bull is in the marsh, his children are hungry, he is with Rachel, I know it, she will have his last penny.* The Egyptian leaned his knife-marked face from his window. The wife of Abrim took one look at him, then turned and wrapped her in night and silence. The Egyptian looked from the stars to a chart he had on the sill. He made comparisons, measurements.

*

The Egyptian is still here. He asks me after breakfast, could he

29

get a guide as far as the border? *I have certain persons to meet in the desert,* said he. In the afternoon he left with Simon, donkey by donkey, a muted going. This was the sole guest today, except for a rout of farm servants and shepherds who lay about the barrel like piglets at the teats of a sow, and sung and uttered filth and (two of them) David a ploughman and Amos a shepherd roared about the alleys after Rachel. They came back with bleeding faces, separate and silent, after midnight. Such scum.

*

My brain is reeling from a press of faces! I had no warning of this. First came two bureaucrats, a Parthian and a Cypriot, bearing Caesar's seal, and a boy with them. *Your best room,* said the Cypriot. (For these chit-bearers you get paid a half-year later.) Then came a little company of clerks with scrolls and ledgers and wax and moneybags and a wolf on a chain. They set up benches in the court-yard. Then — O my God — by every road north and south they came, a horde of hook-noses, hillmen, yokels, they swarmed about the doors, come to pay some tribal tax, filthy thirsty goats. *We'll sleep on the roof,* said some. And others, *Provide beer and bread, never mind blankets.* And Rachel shining among them like a fish in a pool. A measured clash of bronze; a column of soldiers possessed the village. And the lieutenant, *I commandeer six rooms. There are no six rooms,* I said. *I commandeer the whole inn,* he said. The Cypriot stood in the door. *I command-eer the whole inn except for the rooms of Caesar's civil servants,* said the lieutenant. *And the room of the chief clerk,* said the Cypriot, *and the room of my hound, and the room of Eros.* (Eros is their catamite.) Never was such a day in this place. The till rattled, I don't deny it, a hundred throats gargled the new wine. Ditches between here and Hebron will be well dunged.

*

The skin is full of blots and scratchings and bad spellings. Put it down to this — my trade is lighting fires, listening,

30

going with chamber pots, whispering, heating cold porridge; not scrivener's work. Know however, the yokels are back in the hills, poor as goats after the taxes and the revelry. Out of Rachel's room all morning small sweet snores. The clerks are balancing figures in their ledgers, melting wax in small flames. The bureaucrats are playing at chess in their room and sipping the old Chian. Eros, like Rachel, sleeps. The soldiers polish their greaves and drink and throw dice; two of them, bare and bronze-knuckled and bloodied, boxed in the sand at noon. There came a man and a woman from the north to pay the tax, very late, and wanted a room. This was after dark. I had one place, ox and ass kept it warm with winter breathings. I gave the man a lantern.

*

The tax-men have gone, a clash of bronze on one side, a wedge of steel on the other, the Parthian on horseback before, the Cypriot on horseback behind, the wolf chained to the money cart, Eros carried by two black men in a silk chair, swaying aloft like a tulip. The first star brought the shepherds. *The soldiers have drunk all the wine,* I said. Amos stood well back in the shadows. *You,* I said, *Amos, stay outside, never come back. I bar you from this place. You and your punch-ups and your pewkings.* I said sweetly to the others, *The Romans have dried the barrel.* The shepherds drifted on past me. One carried a new white winter lamb.

*

Most secret and urgent. Aaron will bring this on horseback, direct from inn to palace, helter-skelter, a shower of hooves and stars. The negro with the cut cheeks has come back, and with him an Indian and one from very far east with eyes like grass-blades. In the first light they seemed like revellers masked and weary from a carnival. They had men servants with them, heavy baggage on the mules, bales and jars. I lit fires, put out sweet water, spread woven blankets over linen. They went about the

31

village all day with questing eyes. I poked among the baggage — ingots, cruets, chalices, tiaras, candlesticks, swords, thuribles, swathe upon swathe of heavy green silk, emeralds cold as ice. They came back late. They wrote their names in the guest book, steep square letters like Hindu temples, like ships of Cathay. I cannot read it, I have torn out the page for your perusal. *Please*, I said, *to enter places of origin.* Coal Face murmured, *The broken kingdoms of this world,* and wrote in the book. Nothing in the room for a while but shadows and flutters. *Also enter,* I said, *the nature of your business. You understand, the imperial government requires this.* Bronze Face said, *Bearers of precious gifts.* Nothing again — one star that hung a web of glimmers and shadows about the chamber. *Blessings given to men in the beginning,* he went on at last, *that have been wrongly spent, on pomp, wars, usury, whoredoms, vainglory: ill-used heavenly gifts. We no longer know what to do with these mysteries. Our thrones are broken. We have brought the old treasures here by difficult ways. We are looking for the hands that first gave them, in the ancient original kingdom. We will offer them back again. Let them shine now in the ceremonies of the poor.* I lit a cluster of seven candles at the wall. *But first we must find the kingdom,* said Daffodil Face, smiling. *Perhaps this kingdom does not exist. Perhaps we found it and did not recognize it. Perhaps it is hidden so deep in birth and love and death that we will never find it. If so, we will leave our skulls in the desert. We do not know where we should go from here. Perhaps the kingdom is a very simple thing.* I kept my hands clasped and my head to one side. *Landlord,* said Coal Face, *your guests tonight are poor lost cold hungry kings. What have you got for us in your cellar?* I informed them that their rooms were ready. I said that I had bread with honey and currants and dates in it, baked that same morning. I mentioned Rachel. I said also my inn was famous for wines, in keg or skin or flagon. I hoped the gentlemen would enjoy their stay. It was cold, I said, for the time of year. They did not move. The night was a sack of coal with one diamond in it. I turned to the door.

32

RUNES FROM A
HOLY ISLAND

Press-Gang
> A man-of-war enchanted
> Three boys away.
> Pinleg, Windbag, Lord Rum returned.

Hierarchy
> A claret laird,
> Seven fishermen with ploughs,
> Women, beasts, corn, fish, stones.

Harpoonist
> He once riveted boat to whale.
> Frail-fingered now
> He weaves crab prisons.

Wreck
> The *Merle d'Or* struck at Scabra.
> One man flung shoreward,
> Cried strangely, fell.

Books
> No more ballads in Eynhallow.
> The schoolmaster
> Opens a box of grammars.

Skerries
> A fanged treeless island.
> On shipwrecked wood
> Men die, love, cry sunwards.

The Chapel of The Visitation
> Before the unuttered Christstone
> A new arch,
> Two bending women, a stone kiss.

Ruined Chapel
> Among scattered Christ stones
> Devoutly leave
> Torn nets, toothache, winter wombs.

33

Saint
> A starved island, Cormack
> With crossed hands,
> Stones become haddock and loaf.

Easter
> Friday, dayspring, a pealing cockerel.
> Haul west, fishermen,
> With flushed violent mouths.

Lost
> An island without roads.
> Ikey the tinker
> Stood throat-deep in the bog.

Dove and Crow
> A preacher broke our dove-stone.
> Sermons, crowflocks,
> Blackened furrow and shore.

Circle
> Cod, give needles and oil.
> Winter hands
> Must sew shrouds by lamplight.

Fish and Corn
> Our isle is oyster-gray,
> That patched coat
> Is the Island of Horses.

RUNES FROM THE
ISLAND OF HORSES

Winter
> Three winter brightnesses —
> Bridesheet, boy in snow,
> Kirkyard spade.

Barn Dance
> Fiddler to farm-girls, a reel,
> A rose,
> A tumult of opening circles.

Respectability
> Sigurd lay with three women,
> Reckoning his mother
> And thwart twin sister.

Farm Girl
> Spinster, elder, moth
> Quiz till dawn
> The lamp in Merran's window.

Entrances
> Between thief and hoard
> Three narrow doors —
> Furrow, maidenhead, grave.

Kirkyard
> Pennies for eyes, we seek
> Unbearable treasure
> Through a wilderness of skulls.

Mirror
> Ikey unpacked a flat stone.
> It brimmed
> With clouds, buttercups, false smiles.

WHEN YOU ARE OLD

Some night when you are gray
And lonely, by muttering flame
(Closed your sweet womb,
Your breasts fallen away,

The rose of one tremulous day
Haunting that loaded room)
Take up my book with your name,
Turn yellow leaves and say,

'That spring, whatever the parish talk,
We made one blessed rhyme
On a shaken branch of love.
Then the eye of the hawk
Down the huge convex of time
Measured our dove.'

TINKERS

Three princes rigged like scarecrows
Straggled along the shore
And every clucking wife
Ran in and barred her door.

Their coats hung in such shreds
The dogs barked as they came.
O but their steps were a dance,
Their eyes all black flame!

The wife's undone her pack
And spread it at our door.
Grails, emeralds, peacock feathers
Scattered over the floor.

The man flashed his bow,
His fiddle had only one string,
But where is the sun-drowned lark
Like that can sing?

The dark boy wore his rags
Like an April-wakened tree,
Or as a drift of seaweed
Glitters on the arms of the sea.

Princes, they ruled in our street
A long shining age,
While Merran peeped through her curtains
Like a hawk from a cage.

Paupers, they filthied our pier
A piece of one afternoon,
Then scowled, stank, shouldered their packs
And cursed and were gone.

THREE SONGS FROM A PLAY

I

The Ballad of John Barleycorn,
The Ploughman, and the Furrow.

As I was ploughing in my field
The hungriest furrow ever torn
Followed my plough and she did cry
'Have you seen my mate John Barleycorn?'

Says I, 'Has he got a yellow beard?
Is he always whispering night and morn?
Does he up and dance when the wind is high?'
Says she, *'That's my John Barleycorn.*

One day they took a cruel knife
(O, I am weary and forlorn!)
They struck him at his golden prayer.
They killed my priest, John Barleycorn.

They laid him on a wooden cart,
Of all his summer glory shorn,
And threshers broke with stick and stave
The shining bones of Barleycorn.

The miller's stone went round and round,
They rolled him underneath with scorn,
The miller filled a hundred sacks
With the crushed pride of Barleycorn.

A baker came by and bought his dust.
That was a madman, I'll be sworn.
He burned my hero in a rage
Of twisting flames, John Barleycorn.

A brewer came by and stole his heart.
Alas, that ever I was born!
He thrust it in a brimming vat
And drowned my dear John Barleycorn.

38

And now I travel narrow roads,
My hungry feet are dark and worn,
But no-one in this winter world
Has seen my dancer Barleycorn.'

I took a bannock from my bag.
Lord, how her empty mouth did yawn!
Says I, 'Your starving days are done,
For here's your lost John Barleycorn.'

I took a bottle from my pouch,
I poured out whisky in a horn.
Says I, 'Put by your grief, for here
Is the merry blood of Barleycorn.'

She ate, she drank, she laughed, she danced.
And home with me she did return.
By candle light in my old straw bed
She wept no more for Barleycorn.

II

Tinker's Song

'Darst thu gang b' the black furrow
This night, thee and thy song? . . .'
'Wet me mooth wi' the Lenten ale,
I'll go along.'

They spied him near the black furrow
B' the glim o' the wolf star.
Slow the dance was in his feet,
Dark the fiddle he bore.

There stood three men at the black furrow
And one was clad in gray.
No mortal hand had woven that claith
B' the sweet light o' day.

There stood three men at the black furrow
And one was clad in green.
They're taen the fiddler b' the hand
Where he was no more seen.

There stood three men at the black furrow
And one was clad in yellow.
They're led the fiddler through a door
Where never a bird could follow.

They've put the gowd cup in his hand,
Elfin bread on his tongue.
There he bade a hunder years,
Him and his lawless song.

'Darst thu gang through the black furrow
On a mirk night, alone? . . .'
'I'd rather sleep wi' Christen folk
Under a kirkyard stone.'

III

Fiddler's Song

The storm is over, lady.
The sea makes no more sound.
What do you wait for, lady?
His yellow hair is drowned.

The waves go quiet, lady,
Like sheep into the fold.
What do you wait for, lady?
His kissing mouth is cold.

THE WEDDING
GUEST

Hamnavoe of water and granite and sky, at gray daystart I say
farewell to you, I make an end now, in a morning that
is not the morning rising monotonously upon our vanity,
gray out of black, a many thousand beginnings till age
makes of morning a mockery, but in a secret set-apart
morning, a triune welling of dayspring and April and
youth, when fire and earth have their way one with
another, a lovely spurting of seed and egg and spawn, on
such a morning I rose and washed in the rockpool and
said farewell in particular to the *Sigrid*'s fishermen and
left the village before the girls came out to the well for
their water, to the stack for their peats, laughing and lett-
ing on not to look at the strong arms weaving and baiting
the black fish-twine, and went on past the cross at the
end of the village to the summons and the ceremony.

*

As I went north in mid-morning, going near the edge of crags
that are set stark between sea and clouds, slowly walking
and lingering, from shell-strewn ledges stirred the skuas,
strong beautiful birds, and circled, and fell about my head
with threat and thunderclap of wings, so that I seemed
like a man with his head in a confusion of sharp circles,
and on I went with cold bidden blood, and presently
wing and claw and beak faltered and fell away and retur-
ned to the mothering niches, and on my feet went with
no change of pace through the salt-bitten grass, but my
body was a smithy — an assault, a wincing, a tumult of
heart-strokes — and I leaned northwards dutifully into
the wind, and the wind falling folded me in two huge
dove-wings.

*

In the afternoon I came to a place called Yesnaby where the
line of western crags was broken into much confusion of
rock and sea, and there in a sudden green valley locked
from the noise of ocean I blundered across a camp of

41

tinkers, and above a flame one man was shaping a tin cup with a hammer, and a boy drained blood through the throat of a rabbit into the earth, and a young man held a hawk on his wrist and sang sometimes and at other times whispered to the fierce tranced head, and a girl suckled a baby, and an old man and an old woman looked at me as indifferently as if I were a goat, and a child came up glistering out of the sea, and there I would have stopped to warm me a while (these tribes exist pure, birth to death, in a fire of simply pagan lust), but that a far behest lured me towards a consummation so beautiful that we but echo the ecstacy with harps and statues; as the naked tinker boy held now to the shell of his ear a colder sea mouth.

*

Created heart of man, when were you ever clear of sorrow? — at the long beach of Skaill as north I went a huddle of gray shawls watched the sea, for, said a girl, there is one boat, the *Skarf,* that went out this morning and is not come back, and they made confusion of words and wailing, but an old woman stood a little apart from them, a fisherman's mother, and said never a word, but put a withered look on the withered sea — and I tried to comfort them, saying that I too was a fisherman and with the wind northerly and a good shoal of herring off Hoy many a boat would be reaping an Atlantic harvest to give all the parish its wintering of food and oil, and this word was a comfort to them — one gave me a scallop shell to hang at my belt — and they fluttered and mewed about me for a while like white-maas, and only the old one kept silence — but again as I left them their thin eyes prised at the oyster of the horizon.

*

Now I was come to Quoyloo, a cluster of ale houses in a valley at sunset, and each howff was the sprawled body of Barleycorn, the barrel his belly, the lamp his yellow eye, and his servingmen feasting with quarrel and song at his gross undiminished godhead, and slow went

42

my feet past the open door of Sigurd's ale-house where
an old man sat on a lobster-box with pewter and froth
in his whiskers and past Thorfinn's ale-house where a
ploughman sat at a board with sixty-four black-and-white
squares and was silently reflected in a fisherman with
sixty-four white-and-black squares (and by that mirror I
knew the loneliness of man) and past Sweyn's ale-house
where Applecheeks in the door cried out 'Welcome,
traveller' and the smell of his malt came near to ravel the
ordered beads of my intention (*A wedding? Begin here
the bridal, Cana was a feast of jars — Rejoice O young
man in thy youth — Drink thy wine with a merry heart*)
and past the barrels at the end of the house, and out into
the pasture and through a cornfield towards — O most
faint desire now — a ghostly bride cup.

*

Through Marwick I dragged the struggling sack of my lusts.
On I went, a beast-bearing ghost. One star stood over
the hill.

There in a byre door a young woman lingered. She dipped
cup in bucket. She held out white dripping warmth, cow
honey, buttercup ale. My fingers gathered the cup, mouth
lapped milk. She pressed against the doorpost, she gave
me room to pass into the cow-dung darkness, the breath-
ing beasts, a spread of blond straw.

Glint of sea-surf in the thickening light. Woven into the hill
a first strand of sackcloth.

By the old woman's fire of peats I sat; who uttered a parish
litany of deaths, births, espousals, and the changing price
of goose eggs.

A man passed through with a lantern and a mash of old bann-
ocks in a plate, going past into the pigsty.

The old woman knelt, she coughed, she mumbled prayers, she
crossed herself, she eased her body, hand by elbow by
shoulder by head, slowly, on to the rack of the stone
floor, and covered her bones with a hide.

The man came back with a dapple of lantern-and-darkness about his knees. He glowered at me and went out to sleep among the horses.

The old one coughed for a long time, then began to snore softly, her mouth fluttering open and close.

Then came the girl from her making of cheese and butter in the cold room next the sea and stood in the dying light of the peatfire and, garment by garment, unfolded her rose and honey nakedness, faintly and secretely smiling, and lay down with the old woman, spring beside winter, and softly filled the house with buttercup breath.

I stood outside in the yard. Star by star had stepped down to fill its lamp at the sunset. Their cold fires westered slowly. A dog barked in the next farm.

*

Light and sea-noise and soil of Birsay, travelled towards you this guest a many a morning, a many a sin, a many a prayer, yet can he still by no means pass over, he must bide with his feet in a drift of seapinks, for the sea has lain with his two arms about the island all night, and glutted every cave and fissure, and now turns slowly from the island, glutted, and begins to ebb from the island with a sound like a struck harp, and *Lauds* glimmers, a frail hidden monotony, and fades, and sea lapses from crag and shelf, and from seapink to sand to washed rock advances the foot of the pilgrim, and the Bride is hidden in her chamber, she has not yet come forth all glorious in robes of spun gold with many a hand-maiden in her train, and slips from rock the sea (and two brothers drift west in a boat with creels), and *Terce* brightens, and from stone and stone and stone shrinks the sea (and three brothers come out with yoke and ox and plough to a steep half-done furrow) and the Bridegroom is in the sanctuary, hidden, there he abides, his single watch-lamp like ruby or stigma or rose, and sea falters from weed and limpet and sand (and one solitary brother stoops now with a basket among rock-pools) and ocean surges at last clear of the island, and the foot of the bidden one goes cold among seaweed, a slow perilous dance between the cloven waters, and from the steeple the first bronze mouth (struck) brims, mildly they all brim then, the mass-bells (swung) and they quiver, up and down, nuptial summonings, round on round of welcome, *Here is your single cell, here all time is but the lucency of a single morning, prepare here your distillings of the Rose for the kirkyard where lie in light and peace the hundred brothers of Birsay,* and a dozen doves, clustered, query round the slipway, and enfold him, and out at sea a raven sail, wind laden, westward urgently leans.

Poems from
LOAVES AND FISHES

THE OLD WOMEN

Go sad or sweet or riotous with beer
Past the old women gossiping by the hour,
They'll fix on you from every close and pier
An acid look to make your veins run sour.

"No help," they say, "his grandfather that's dead
Was troubled with the same dry-throated curse,
And many a night he made the ditch his bed.
This blood comes welling from the same cracked source."

On every kind of merriment they frown.
But I have known a gray-eyed sober boy
Sail to the lobsters in a storm, and drown.
Over his body dripping on the stones
Those same old hags would weave into their moans
An undersong of terrible holy joy.

THE DEATH OF PETER ESSON

Tailor, Town Librarian, Free Kirk Elder

Peter at some immortal cloth, it seemed,
Fashioned and stitched, for so long had he sat
Heraldic on his bench. We never dreamed
It was his shroud that he was busy at.

Well Peter knew, his thousand books would pass
Gray into dust, that still a tinker's tale
As hard as granite and as sweet as grass,
Told over reeking pipes, outlasts them all.

The Free Kirk cleaves gray houses — Peter's ark
Freighted for heaven, galeblown with psalm and prayer.
The predestined needle quivered on the mark.
The wheel spun true. The seventieth rock was near.

Peter, I mourned. Early on Monday last
There came a wave and stood above your mast.

THE MASQUE OF BREAD

What answer would he give, now he had reached
The Inquisitor's door, down seventy hungry streets,
Each poorer than the last, the last a slum
Rambling like nightmare round his winter feet?

The Inquisitor's door? The walls were all blank there,
But a white bakehouse with a little arch
And a creaking sign . . . Against the fragrant doorpost
He clung, like drifted snow, while the shuttered oven
Opened on hills of harvest sun and corn.

The loaf the bakers laid on the long shelf
Was bearded, thewed, goldcrusted like a god.
Each drew a mask over his gentle eyes
— Masks of the wolf, the boar, the hawk, the reaper —
And in mock passion clawed the bread.
                        But he
Who stood between the cold Plough and the embers
In the door of death, knew that this masquerade
Was a pure seeking past a swarm of symbols,
The millwheel, sun, and scythe, and ox, and harrow,
Station by station to that simple act
Of terror or love, that broke the hill apart.
But what stood there — an Angel with a sword
Or Grinning Rags — astride the kindled seed?

He knelt in the doorway. Still no question came
And still he knew no answer.
                        The bread lay broken,
Fragmented light and song.
                        When the first steeple
Shook out petals of morning, long bright robes
Circled in order round the man that died.

THORFINN

Sing Thorfinn's drowning.
          Tired of his thieving guests,
The kestrel shape that wore his hand and eye,
The stealthy-by-moon deep-litter ghost,
And the seducer of vagrant Pertelotes,
Clad in his innocent hungers Thorfinn walked
Past farmyards havering with hens and greed.

Through streets of finger-pointing folk who'd set
Iron bars between him and the sun
(They shackled not the spectre but the boy)
Went Thorfinn to the clean curve of the oar.

Heart sick of the land
Where troubles grew with every grass blade
And every rose gushed from a septic root
And every casual car was the Black Maria,

He rowed his little boat behind the holm
To take the purple samurai of the flood.
Cornless they range, the lobsters.
By weeded rock and plangent pool
God puts in their beautiful claws
Sweet algae and tiny glimmering fish
The dropping surfeits of the rich Atlantic
Ravelling its rivers through the corn-patched Orkneys
And shrinking, twice a day.
(To their peril they eat man fodder:
Explore a casual fishgut hole, they're snared
In a tarry mesh, drawn up, and drowned with air.)

Whether it chanced, the Owner of these lobsters,
Grown sour at Thorfinn as any bristling poultry man
Turned a salt key in his last door of light;

Or whether Love, abroad in a seeking wave
Lifted him from the creaking rowlocks of time
And flung a glad ghost on a wingless shore:

No one can tell.
          A crofter at early light

Found an empty boat stuttering on the rocks
And dawn-cold cocks cheering along the links.

GREGORY HERO

Five suns lit his dust.
They're out, and for his death
We yield him images: he was
A Viking ship, a white stallion.

Twelve winds knit his strength
From fish, corn, old gravestones.
Twenty years stored his veins
With spindrift, rain, the milk
Of vanished women's mildness and the kegs
Of courage smuggled down generations.

Gregory dispersed again, down the
Throats of crabs, spun through
Long green currents of water,
Sunk to the root of seaweed and
In core of shells settled.

Tall virgins, stretching hand and breast
To catch the sun and sweet showers,
Mending nets or in the cornfield
Taking a burnish and caress of wind,
It's Gregory pursues you round the world.

PORT OF VENUS

The holy earl, his kestrel pilgrimage
Hardly begun, furled sails in a strange port
Out of the kick of the gale and the salt siege,
And all the sailors called for a night's sport

With foreign girls and ale, eyeing their lord,
Ignorant of what sanctities he planned —
Unlock the city granaries with his sword,
Or lay a cold mouth on the prince's hand

To get fresh corn aboard his famished ships.
The square was mild with doves. The elders came
And led this hawkwing, in a barnyard choir,
To greet their prince, a girl with snooded hair
And shy cold breasts. They trembled as their lips
Welded holy and carnal in one flame.

THE STRANGER

One night he stayed with us
(Said the tall proud woman)
One night in our poor house
And then mounted his mare
And clattered thankless forth.
I've thought him ever since
A great one of the earth
— A poet or a prince —
Touched with unlucky fire.

That night when I was laid
(Sang the milking girl)
Sound in my box bed
He broke upon my rest
And in the deep midnight
Turned that first cruel pain
Into a wild delight
That buds and flowers again
When his child seeks my breast.

What was he but a tink
(Cried the obstinate man)
All rags, blether, and stink?
Yet when he slouched through that door
Begging a slice of bread
And a drop of ale in a glass
The old wife bowed her head,
And a throb went through our lass
As though an angel stood there.

HAMNAVOE

My father passed with his penny letters
Through closes opening and shutting like legends
        When barbarous with gulls
        Hamnavoe's morning broke

On the salt and tar steps. Herring boats,
Puffing red sails, the tillers
        Of cold horizons, leaned
        Down the gull-gaunt tide

And threw dark nets on sudden silver harvests.
A stallion at the sweet fountain
        Dredged water, and touched
        Fire from steel-kissed cobbles.

Hard on noon four bearded merchants
Past the pipe-spitting pier-head strolled,
        Holy with greed, chanting
        Their slow grave jargon.

A tinker keened like a tartan gull
At cuithe-hung doors. A crofter lass
        Trudged through the lavish dung
        In a dream of cornstalks and milk.

In "The Artic Whaler" three blue elbows fell,
Regular as waves, from beards spumy with porter,
        Till the amber day ebbed out
        ·To its black dregs.

The boats drove furrows homeward, like ploughmen
In blizzards of gulls. Gaelic fisher girls
        Flashed knife and dirge
        Over drifts of herring,

And boys with penny wands lured gleams
From the tangled veins of the flood. Houses went blind
        Up one steep close, for a
        Grief by the shrouded nets.

The kirk, in a gale of psalms, went heaving through
A tumult of roofs, freighted for heaven. And lovers
    Unblessed by steeples, lay under
    The buttered bannock of the moon.

He quenched his lantern, leaving the last door.
Because of his gay poverty that kept
    My seapink innocence
    From the worm and black wind;

And because, under equality's sun,
All things wear now to a common soiling,
    In the fire of images
    Gladly I put my hand
    To save that day for him.

HALCRO

Don't go to that old man
With daffodil-shining dove-winged words
To hang beside his clock.
His wall is wild with ships and birds.

Even the rum you bring
And the tobacco coiled and mellow
He loves to chew, he'll stuff
In the oblivion of his pillow.

Give him the salty texts
Chanted in smithy, pub, and loan —
How the corn's ripening; how
The pier was gray with Grimsbymen

Last stormy weekend; how
Sigurd got a pint of stout
So riotously sour
They had to call the police out;

And how Grieg's spindly lass
With hollow neck and freckled brow
Is suddenly grown a woman
And has two breasts like roses now . . .

Then see his bone-bright hands
Frail on the chair, grow firm again
In the stillness of old brawls,
Torn nets, sweet dust, and tangled grain.

THE LODGING

The stones of the desert town
Flush; and, a star-filled wave,
Night steeples down.

From a pub door here and there
A random ribald song
Leaks on the air.

The Roman in a strange land
Broods, wearily leaning
His lance in the sand.

The innkeeper over the fire
Counting his haul, hears not
The cry from the byre;

But rummaging in the till
Grumbles at the drunken shepherds
Dancing on the hill;

And wonders, pale and grudging,
If the queer pair below
Will pay their lodging.

THE HEAVENLY STONES

Three men came to our door with gifts
When I was a lightsome lad.
Yellow and red and black they stood
Against the milking shed.

"Will you take the sign of wealth?" said one
And give me a disc of gold,
The same with which God's corn and wine
Are dearly bought and sold.

I ran with it to the midden heap
And sank it in that filth.
"If that's how you treat good gold," laughed he,
"You lock the door on wealth."

The red one said, "My jar's sweet fume
Is sensuality."
What sound was that? My father's boar
Rutting behind the stye.

I tilted the vessel with my foot
Till the dark oil shimmered out.
"If that's how you treat the dancing five,
Go wear a beggar's clout;

"Who might have had heraldic cloaks
Over your shoulder slung,
And bedded with more beautiful girls
Than ever Solomon sung."

The third old man came shuffling up,
And opened his earthen bottle:
"O what are breast and thigh but dust,
And what is yellow metal?

"Taste the bitters in my cruse,
Nor twist your face, my son.
This has grown on the tree of life
Since Adam's day began.

"And you must hang on your own tree
Watered with women's tears,

The grape of God that ripens slow
Through forty hundred years.

"The men of dust will pluck you down
And eat your flesh for food,
And angel fingered, fill their flasks
At the five gates of your blood.

"Drink this wine now, that you may know
What Adam had to suffer,
And what atonement, on that day,
A son of God must offer" . . .

I longed to spit it from my mouth
But yet I drank it down
With anguish, and the three old men
Rode onward to the town.

That hour I felt mortality
Fasten about my bones.
The gold out of the midden sang
And heaven leaked from the stones.

The shaken branch, The Voice, the draped
Whispering coil of flame,
And Eve a tall unfingered harp
Strung with desire and shame.

All the world's honey and its dust
Through my five senses falling . . .
Till from the hearth stone where she knelt
I heard my mother calling,

And heard my father's restless saw
Rasping through the wood —
Old craftsman, making crib and cross
Where simple trees had stood.

A Roman column under the moon
Passed like a gleaming wave
That time would scatter, each bright drop
To its salt separate grave.

I flung away the heavenly stones
Yellow and black and red
That I had played with all day long
And, laughing, crept to bed.

THE EXILE

So, blinded with Love
He tried to blunder
Out of that field
Of floods and thunder.

The frontiers were closed.
At every gate
The sworded pitiless
Angels wait.

There's no retreat.
The path mounts higher
And every summit
Fringed with fire.

The night is blind,
Dark winds, dark rains:
But now his blood
Pours through his veins,

His hammer heart
Thuds in his breast
"What love devises,
That is best,"

And he would not turn,
Though the further side
Dowered his days
With fame and pride.

What though his feet
Are hurt and bare?
Love walks with him
In the menacing air.

The frontiers sealed;
His foot on the stone;
And low in the East
The gash of dawn.

ELEGY

The Magnustide long swords of rain
   Quicken the dust. The ploughman turns
     Furrow by holy furrow
      The liturgy of April.
     What rock of sorrow
   Checks the seed's throb and flow
Now the lark's skein is thrown
      About the burning sacrificial hill?

Cold exiles from that ravished tree
   (Fables and animals guard it now)
     Whose reconciling leaves
      Fold stone, cornstalk and lark,
     Our first blood grieves
   That never again her lips
Flowering with song we'll see,
      Who, winged and bright, speeds down into
       the dark.

Now let those risers from the dead,
   Cornstalks, golden conspirators,
     Cry on the careless wind
      Ripeness and resurrection;
     How the calm wound
   Of the girl entering earth's side
Gives back immortal bread
      For this year's dust and rain that shall be man.

CHAPEL BETWEEN CORNFIELD
AND SHORE

Above the ebb, that gray uprooted wall
Was arch and chancel, choir and sanctuary,
A solid round of stone and ritual.
Knox brought all down in his wild hogmanay.

The wave turns round. New ceremonies will thrust
From the thrawn acre where those good stones bleed
Like corn compelling sun and rain and dust
After the crucifixion of the seed.

Restore to that maimed rockpool, when the flood
Sounds all her lucent strings, its ocean dance;
And let the bronze bell nod and cry above
Ploughshare and creel; and sieged with hungry sins
A fisher priest offer our spindrift bread
For the hooked hands and harrowed heart of love.

DAFFODILS

Heads skewered with grief
Three Marys at the cross
(Christ was wire and wax
festooned on a dead tree)

Guardians of the rock,
their emerald tapers touch
the pale wick of the sun
and perish before the rose
bleeds on the solstice stone
and the cornstalk unloads
peace from hills of thorn

Spindrifting blossoms
from the gray comber of March
thundering on the world,
splash our rooms coldly with
first grace of light, until
the corn-tides throb, and fields
drown in honey and fleeces

Shawled in radiance
tissue of sun and snow
three bowl-bound daffodils
in the euclidian season
when darkness equals light
and the world's circle shudders
down to one bleeding point
Mary Mary and Mary
triangle of grief.

Poems from
THE YEAR OF THE WHALE

Because of his long pilgrimage
     From pub to alehouse
          And all the liquor laws he'd flout,
Being under age
          And wringing peatbog spirit from a clout
Into a secret kettle,
          And making every Sabbath a carouse,
Mansie brought a twelve-year bottle.

Because his shy foot turned aside
     From Merran's door,
          And Olga's coat with the red button
And Inga's side
          Naked as snow or swan or wild bog cotton
Made him laugh loud
          And after, spit with scunner on the floor,
Marget sewed a long chaste shroud.

Because the scythe was in the oats
     When he lay flat,
          And Jean Macdonald's best March ale
Cooled the long throats
          (At noon the reapers drank from the common pail)
And Sanders said
          'Corn enough here for every tramp and rat',
Sigrid baked her lightest bread.

Although the fleet from Hamnavoe
     Drew heavy nets
          Off Noup Head, in a squall of rain,
Turning in slow
          Gull-haunted circles near the three-mile line,
And mouthing cod
          Went iced and salted into slippery crates,
One skipper heard and bowed his head.

Because at Dounby and the fair
     Twelve tearaways
          Brought every copper in the islands

Round their uproar
    And this one made a sweet and sudden silence
Like that white bird
    That broke the tempest with a twig of praise,
The preacher spoke the holy word.

Because the hour of grass is brief
    And the red rose
        Is a bare thorn in the east wind
And a strong life
        Runs out and spends itself like barren sand
And the dove dies
    And every lovliest lilt must have a close,
Old Betsy came with bitter cries.

Because his dance was gathered now
    And parish feet
        Went blundering their separate roads
After the plough
        And after net and peat and harvest loads,
Yet from the cradle
    Their fated steps with a fixed passion beat,
Tammas brought his Swedish fiddle.

SHIPWRECK

Paul grounded at Braga, a gull on his shoulder.
The milkmaids wrung him dry.
He lay that night at the fire of Lifia
And then moved inland
And keeps pigs on a black hill.
    Jan put a cut of tobacco in his teeth
When the *Maggi* struck.
They found him at the end of the kirk
Near dawn, out of the gale,
Squirting poison among the tombstones.
    For Gregory was much grief in the crofts.
The sea did not offer him with green hands
To the seven dark shawls.
His bones fouled no net or slipway.
With small diagonals crabs covered them.
    Two storms and a dove later
A man with a limpet pail
Turned a gold swathe among seaweed.
That was the hair
Of Robin, weaver of nets, in a warp of ebb.
    Peero said when the first lump of salt
Fell through wrenched timbers,
'Now it seems I can never
Hang a brass chain at my belly
Or sit in the council
Or go among doors with the holy cards' . . .
The gray lumps fell and fell and stopped his breath.
    Peter was three years getting home from the wreck.
He found his feet at Houton.
The ale house there kept him a week.
He stayed at Gair for harvest,
Drowned and drunk again with broken corn,
Then shipped at Scapa
For the blue fish, the whales, the Davis Straits
And casks of hellfire Arctic rum.
He stood dry in his door at last.
Merrag wore a black shawl.

71

He read his own tombstone that evening.
    For Donald the way was not long.
His father had a dozen horse at Skaill
But Donald loved the dark net.
Indeed for Donald the day and the way were not long.
The old men said,
'Such skill at Greek and physics and poetry
Will bring this Donald fame at last'.
But for him the day was not long.
His day was this long —
Sixteen years, four months, and two days.

CULLODEN: *The Last Battle*

The black cloud crumbled.
        My plaid that Morag wove
In Drumnakeil, three months before the eagle
Fell in the west, curled like the gray sea hag
Around my blood.
        We crouched on the long moor
And broke our last round bannock.
        Fergus Mor
Was praying to every crossed and beaded saint
That swung Iona, like the keel of Scotland,
Into the wrecking European wave.
Gow shook his flask. Alastair sang out
They would be drunker yet on German blood
Before the hawk was up. For 'Look', he cried,
'At all the hogsheads waiting to be tapped
Among the rocks' . . .
        Old iron-mouth spilled his brimstone,
Nodded and roared. Then all were at their texts,
And Fergus fell, and Donald gave a cry
Like a wounded stag, and raised his steel and ran
Into the pack.
        But we were hunters too,
All smoking tongues. I picked my chosen quarry
Between the squares. Morag at her wheel
Turning the fog of wool to a thin swift line
Of August light, drew me to love no surer
Than that red man to war. And his cold stance
Seemed to expect my coming. We had hastened
Faithful as brothers from the sixth cry of God
To play this game of ghost on the long moor.
His eyes were hard as dice, his cheek was cropped
For the far tryst, his Saxon bayonet
Bright as a wolf's tooth. Our wild paths raced together,
Locked in the heather, faltered by the white stone,
Then mine went on alone.
        'Come back, come back',
Alastair cried.

I turned.
                    Three piercing shapes
Drifted about me in the drifting smoke.
We crossed like dreams.
                    This was the last battle.
We had not turned before.

                    The eagle was up
And away to the Isles.
                    That night we lay
Far in the west. Alastair died in the straw.
We travelled homeward, on the old lost roads,
Twilight by twilight, shepherd by weeping shepherd.

My three wounds were heavy and round as medals
Till Morag broke them with her long fingers.

Weaving, she sings of the beauty of defeat.

HORSEMAN AND SEALS

On the green holm they built their church.
There were three arches.
They walked to the village across the ebb.
From this house they got milk.
A farmer cut and carted their peats.
On their rock
Fishermen left a basket of mouthing silver.
They brought the gifts of heaven
To the new children and the suffering shapes.
They returned to the island
And mixed their bell with the seven sounds of the sea.
Eight times a day
They murmured their psalms in that gray place.

A horseman stood at the shore, his feet in seaweed.
He could not cross over.
The sea lay round the holm, a bright girdle.
His voice scattered in the vastness
Though from shore to shore pierced cries of gull and petrel.
What did the horseman want?
Perhaps an old man in the parish was sick,
Or he wanted a blessing on his ship,
Or he wished to argue a point in theology.
From shore to shore they blessed him.
They trooped under the arch for nones.
After the psalms the horseman was still there,
Patient in the seaweed.
The sea shone higher round the skerry.
And the abbot said, 'Cormac, you are the carpenter,
A blessëd occupation.
And tomorrow you will beg some boards and nails
And you will build a little boat,
So that we do not need to keep horsemen waiting on the
     other shore
Who are in need of God' . . .

And while the boat was building under the crag
Paul gathered whelks.
From the cold triangular pools he gathered handfulls
And put them in his basket.
He sang *Dominus Pascit Me*, gathering whelks.
Twenty seals lay on the skerry.
They turned their faces towards the psalm.
The brother sang for them also,
For the seals with their beautiful gentle old men's faces.
Then the ebb subtracted one sound
From the seven-fold harmony of ocean.
The tide lay slack, between ebb and flowing, a slipped girdle.
Paul gathered whelks and sang
Till the flood set in from the west, with a sound like harps,
And one by one the seals entered the new water.

THE ABBOT

Here at Innertun we have seven brothers.
Havard was a shepherd
In Hoy, that huddle of blue shoulders.
In the tavern there
He broke the back of a loud fisherman.
He has given his fifty sheep to the widow,
To the three orphans his green hill.
At Innertun now, he weaves our coats.

At Rinansay, Einar was a butterfly
Over a tangled harp.
The girls miss him in that low island.
Now when candles are lit
For matins, in the warp of winter,
He drifts, our gray moth
Among the woven monotonies of God.

Sigurd sailed to Iceland, a boy,
And lost an arm there.
He was with Leif on the Greenland voyage.
He bought a Galway horse, sire of thirty
And sailed home from Norway
With tusks of walrus, proper embellishment
For hilt and helmet and ale-cup.
'Too old now', said Sigurd
'For any port but the blue of heaven,
I teach the brothers shipwit.'

We have a field at Innertun
That was full of stones last April.
Plenty of lobsters and milk
At our fasting tables.
Then Erling rode from Birsay, love-torn.
He laid a plough on our acre.
He gives us bannocks and new ale.

You would not wish to have seen
The *Gothenberg* at the crag
Like a hare in the cold jaw of a wolf.
You would not wish to have seen

Seagulls over blind shapes on the sand.
From the timbers we made a new door
And the Swedish boy
Has Latin enough to answer the priest now.

Rolf whistled down the wild hawk.
He brought twelve free stallions
From the hill Greenay,
Gale shapes, to the horse fair at Hamnavoe.
He put a ring in the bull's nose,
And said in a circle of drunk whalers
'There is a time to finish with beasts
And to strive with angels'.
His knee was among our knees next morning.

This day is a day of sheaves at Innertun
And five sharp circles.
A yellow wind walks on the hill.
The small boats in the Sound
Pluck this brightness and that from their nets.
Our cow watched a black field in March,
And the green tumults of summer.
Today she cries over a sudden radiance,
The clean death of corn.
Christ, crofter, lay kindly on this white beard
Thy sickle, flail, millstone, keg, oven . . . .
They shout across the broken gold.
The boy has found a lark's nest in the oats.

THE POET

Therefore he no more troubled the pool of silence
But put on mask and cloak,
Strung a guitar
And moved among the folk.
Dancing they cried,
'Ah, how our sober islands
Are gay again, since this blind lyrical tramp
Invaded the Fair!'

Under the last dead lamp
When all the dancers and masks had gone inside
His cold stare
Returned to its true task, interrogation of silence.

FARM LABOURER

'God, am I not dead yet?' said Ward, his ear
    Meeting another dawn.
        A blackbird, lost in leaves, began to throb
And on the pier
            The gulls stretched barbarous throats
            Over the creels, the haddock lines, the boats.
        His mortal pain
            All day hung tangled in that lyrical web.

'Seventy years I've had of this', said Ward,
    'Going in winter dark
        To feed the horse, a lantern in my fist,
Snow in my beard,
            Then thresh in the long barn
            Bread and ale out of the skinflint corn,
        And such-like work!'
            And a lark flashed its needle down the west.

OLD FISHERMAN WITH GUITAR

A formal exercise for withered fingers.
   The head is bent,
      The eyes half closed, the tune
Lingers
      And beats, a gentle wing the west had thrown
     Against his breakwater wall with salt savage lament.

So fierce and sweet the song on the plucked string,
   Know now for truth
      Those hands have cut from the net
The strong
      Crab-eaten corpse of Jock washed from a boat
     One old winter, and gathered the mouth of Thora to his
        mouth.

THE YEAR OF THE WHALE

The old go, one by one, like guttered flames.
   This past winter
      Tammag the bee-man has taken his cold blank mask
      To the honeycomb under the hill,
         Corston who ploughed out the moor
      Unyoked and gone; and I ask,
  Is Heddle lame, that in youth could dance and saunter
         A way to the chastest bed?
The kirkyard is full of their names
         Chiselled in stone. Only myself and Yule
         In the ale-house now, speak of the great whale year.

This one and that provoked the taurine waves
   With an arrogant pass,
      Or probing deep through the snow-burdened hill
      Resurrected his flock,
         Or passed from fiddles to ditch
      By way of the quart and the gill,
  All night lay tranced with corn, but stirred to face
         The brutal stations of bread;
While those who tended their lives
         Like sacred lamps, chary of oil and wick,
         Died in the fury of one careless match.

Off Scabra Head the lookout sighted a school
   At the first light.
      A meagre year it was, limpets and crows
      And brief mottled grain.
         Everything that could float
      Circled the school. Ploughs
Wounded those wallowing lumps of thunder and night.
         The women crouched and prayed.
Then whale by whale by whale
         Blundering on the rock with its red stain
         Crammed our winter cupboards with oil and meat.

TROUT FISHER

Semphill, his hat stuck full of hooks
   Sits drinking ale
      Among the English fishing visitors,
   Probes in detail
         Their faults in casting, reeling, selection of flies.
'Never', he urges, 'do what it says in the books'.
      Then they, obscurely wise,
     Abandon by the loch their dripping oars
And hang their throttled tarnish on the scale.

'Forgive me, every speckled trout',
   Says Semphill then,
     'And every swan and eider on these waters.
   Certain strange men
      Taking advantage of my poverty
Have wheedled all my subtle loch-craft out
     So that their butchery
    Seem fine technique in the ear of wives and daughters.
   And I betray the loch for a white coin'.

THE TWELVE PIERS OF HAMNAVOE

Those huge apostle feet
Stand in the ebb.
        Twice daily
The god of whale and iceberg
Returns with gulls
To lay green blessings on them

Or spreads his wounds around
Threatening the nets

Or like an old blind ghost
Folds them in love and lost voices.

HAMNAVOE MARKET

They drove to the Market with ringing pockets.

Folster found a girl
Who put wounds on his face and throat,
Small and diagonal, like red doves.

Johnston stood beside the barrel.
All day he stood there.
He woke in a ditch, his mouth full of ashes.

Grieve bought a balloon and a goldfish.
He swung through the air.
He fired shotguns, rolled pennies, ate sweet fog from a stick.

Heddle was at the Market also.
I know nothing of his activities.
He is and always was a quiet man.

Garson fought three rounds with a negro boxer,
And received thirty shillings,
Much applause, and an eye loaded with thunder.

Where did they find Flett?
They found him in a brazen circle,
All flame and blood, a new Salvationist.

A gypsy saw in the hand of Halcro
Great strolling herds, harvests, a proud woman.
He wintered in the poorhouse.

They drove home from the Market under the stars
Except for Johnston
Who lay in a ditch, his mouth full of dying fires.

COUNTRY GIRL

I make seven circles, my love
For your good breaking.
I make the gray circle of bread
And the circle of ale
And I drive the butter round in a golden ring
And I dance when you fiddle
And I turn my face with the turning sun till your
    feet come in from the field.
My lamp throws a circle of light,
Then you lie for an hour in the hot unbroken
    circle of my arms.

WEATHER BESTIARY

RAIN
The unicorn melts through his prism. Sodden hooves
Have deluged the corn with light.

WIND
A fisherman wets his finger. The eyelash
Of the gray stallion flicks his blood with cold.

SUN
A hard summer. The month I sat at the rock
One fish rose, belly up, a dead gleam.

THUNDER
Corn, lobster, fleece hotly harvested — now
That whale stranded on the blue rock!

FROST
Stiff windless flower, hearse-blossom,
Show us the brightness of blood, stars, apples.

FOG
The sun-dipped isle was suddenly a sheep
Lost and stupid, a dense wet tremulous fleece.

SNOW
Autumn, a moulted parrot, eyes with terror
This weird white cat. It drifts the rose-bush under.

THE HAWK

On Sunday the hawk fell on Bigging
   And a chicken screamed
   Lost in its own little snowstorm.
And on Monday he fell on the moor
   And the Field Club
   Raised a hundred silent prisms.
And on Tuesday he fell on the hill
   And the happy lamb
   Never knew why the loud collie straddled him.
And on Wednesday he fell on a bush
   And the blackbird
   Laid by his little flute for the last time.
And on Thursday he fell on Cleat
   And peerie Tom's rabbit
   Swung in a single arc from shore to hill.
And on Friday he fell on a ditch
   But the rampant rat,
   That eye and that tooth, quenched his flame.
And on Saturday he fell on Bigging
   And Jock lowered his gun
   And nailed a small wing over the corn.

THE IMAGE IN THE HILLS

Language, open the sacred quarry.
   Pagan in clouds, a stone image,
She guards the field, the river, the birds.

The dark hills roll across her silence.
   Beyond their scars and tumults, she sees
A blond morning of honey and fleeces.

Build an arch of hard square words.
   April flows from her wounded hands.
The gentle beasts and legends gather.

Carved on broken stone, at the well
   A stag runs, hard in light, before
The fading tangle of hound and horn.

Stone and litany fold her now.
   Stand in the poem, nude cold girl,
Till the Word wakes and all stones die.

THE CONDEMNED WELL

Turgid, sweet. The well on the brae
Wet fifteen mouths all summer.
To the sisters of Scorran
The well was lover, the water kisses and secrets.
Shall we mention Linky the tailor
Who stitched that silk through his rum?
We shall not forget that drunken cross-legs.
The horse of Quoygarth
Raised there an ecstatic streaming skull,
With square barbarous teeth, black curling lips!
This was the theatre
When Coghill, hotly pursued
By lawyer, creditor, lover
Drenched his deliberate throat with death.
Shall any complain
Because a golden bee hung here
For his tiny ration?
Fool, thou poet, thou rememberest
Ada and Mary and Ann
Who sank bright buckets here.
Poet, those were beautiful girls
Nor could thy net of words hold one.
All these, certainly more,
Drank from that rocky breast,
For always were tinkers passing
And flies that drown
And raging Sabbath thirsts from the ship beyond.
Fool, thou poet,
Tomorrow is the day of the long lead pipe.

THE SAILOR, THE OLD WOMAN, AND THE GIRL

'Have you any help', cried the young sailor
Pulling against the tide,
'Have you any spell or herb to mend
This new pain in my side?'

The old woman gathering whelks
Raised her fierce gray head.
'The best cure in the world for that
Is, take her to your bed.

If watchdogs howl, there's two good places
To end a lover's moans —
The alehouse with its lamp and barrel,
The kirkyard with its stones.

Or use the black worm of the mind.
Think, when she leans up close
And all the lurings of Delilah
Break open like a rose

Against your eyes and throat and mouth,
That I am lying there,
Time's first lover stark as a thorn
In a white winter air'.

The girl sang from another shore
And the tranced oars beat on,
And the old woman's fingers went
Like roots through the gray stone.

HARALD,

the Agnostic Ale-Drinking Shepherd, Enemy
of Ploughmen and Elders and all the
Dancing Sons of Barleycorn, Walks
over the Sabbath Hill to the Shearing

Two bells go pealing through my age,
Two mad majestic criers.
One celebrates the pastured saints,
One descants on hell fires.
They storm at me with trembling mouths
And both of them are liars.

The barman had a little bell
That swayed my soul to peace
At ten last night.
             When the mad horns
Raged in the barley lees,
From lip to bottom of my glass
Clung a shining fleece.

IKEY ON THE PEOPLE OF HELLYA

Rognvald who stalks round Corse with his stick
I do not love.
His dog has a loud sharp mouth.
The wood of his door is very hard.
Once, tangled in his barbed wire
(I was paying respects to his hens, stroking a wing)
He laid his stick on me.
That was out of a hard forest also.

Mansie at Quoy is a biddable man.
Ask for water, he gives you rum.
I strip his scarecrow April by April.
Ask for a scattering of straw in his byre
He lays you down
Under a quilt as long and light as heaven.
Then only his raging woman spoils our peace.

Gray the fisherman is no trouble now
Who quoted me the vagrancy laws
In a voice slippery as seaweed under the kirkyard.
I rigged his boat with the seven curses.
Occasionally still, for encouragement,
I put the knife in his net.

Though she has black peats and a yellow hill
And fifty silken cattle
I do not go near Merran and her cats.
Rather break a crust on a tombstone.
Her great-great-grandmother
Wore the red coat at Gallowsha.

The thousand rabbits of Hollandsay
Keep Simpson's corn short,
Whereby comes much cruelty, gas and gunshot.
Tonight I have lit a small fire.
I have stained my knife red.
I have peeled a round turnip.
And I pray the Lord
To preserve those nine hundred and ninety nine innocent

Finally in Folscroft lives Jeems,
Tailor and undertaker, a crosser of limbs,
One tape for the living and the dead.
He brings a needle to my rags in winter,
And he guards, against my stillness
The seven white boards
I got from the Danish wreck one winter.

THE SEVEN HOUSES

In Memory of John F. Kennedy

Man, you are at the first door,
The woman receives you.
The woman takes you in.
With joy she takes you in to her long hall.
The nine candles are burning.
Here with reptile and fish and beast
You dance in silence.
Here is the table with the first food.
This is the House of the Womb.

Man, you are at the second door.
A woman receives you.
With brief hands she holds you.
She delivers you into time,
Into light and into darkness,
Into sound and silence and a new dance.
From an outer spring
The natural water comes to your mouth.
Also on your head
A man lays seven bright drops.
This is the House of Birth.

Man, you are at the third door.
A tree in a gray courtyard.
Here the animals dare not enter.
The tree is loaded with apples.
Three women stand at the tree,
The bare bitter bloody tree.
With oil and cloths they stand at the tortured tree.
This is the House of Man.

Man, you are at the fourth door.
Ploughman, merchant, engineer
Cross in a busy street.
On the seven oceans beyond
The ships sail on,
The peoples exchanging oil and wheat and music.

The cornstalk is tall in the field.
Through those yellow tides, that peace,
One woman comes,
On her shoulder a tall jar of untasted wine.
This is the House of Corn and Grape.

Man, you are at the fifth door.
The woman has brought you to her gate.
You have drunk her wine.
She has washed your hands at the threshold.
Now she prepares a bed.
Under the seven stars you watch and wait.
Inside, flames twist and untwist their hair.
This is the House of Love.

Man, you are at the sixth door.
The enemies with sculptured faces,
Stiffly they dance
About the disordered dangerous board.
The broken pitcher spills its oil.
Dark at the wall
The harp is a tangle of strings.
The hungry sit at a narrow table
And the Golden Man
Summons another beast from the flames.
The negro hangs on his tree.
At the sixth wall
In growing darkness, you lit one lamp.
This is the House of Policy.

Man, you are at the last door.
Three small mad venomous birds
Define in your skull
A new territory of silence.
The darkness staggered.
Seventy thousand ordered days
Lay ravelled in the arms of a woman.
In a concord of grief
The enemies laid aside their masks,
And later resumed them

For epitaph, platitude, anger.
What they say is of small importance.
Through the arrogance of atom and planet
May the lamp still burn
And bread be broken at the tables of poor men
(The heads bowed
And the sweet shape of the dove at the door.)
This is the House of History.